# Grace for the Grieving
## Words of Comfort in Times of Loss

*Grace for the Grieving—Words of Comfort in Times of Loss*
Compiled by Gordon S. Jackson

Copyright 2022 by Gordon S. Jackson. All rights reserved.
No part of this anthology may be copied or in any way
disseminated to others without the explicit written consent of
the compiler.

All Scripture quotations, unless noted otherwise, are taken
from *The Holy Bible: New International Version (NIV)* ©1973,
1978, 1984, 2011 by Biblica Inc. Used by permission. All
rights reserved worldwide.

# Grace for the Grieving
## Words of Comfort in Times of Loss

Gordon S. Jackson

# INTRODUCTION

With death there is the pain of loss, the pain of separation, and there is the promise of eternal life, and the two things can't be separated.

— Frances Dominica

Death unsparingly pours out hurt upon Christians and non-Christians alike. Yet for the Christian, death ushers in a peculiar paradox. While we too grieve and ache from our loss and separation as much as others, we have a unique view of death—and a unique conviction. That's because Christians of all traditions and denominations, whether Protestant, Catholic or Orthodox, share the profound belief that in death our loved ones have entered eternal life, spared of further hurt or suffering and never to be separated from the presence of God himself.

The Christian view of death thus brings to a grieving soul these things: comfort, hope, an assurance that God is indeed in control, and a promise. The Lord himself, as we see throughout Scripture and especially in the Psalms, aches with us when we ache, and weeps beside us when we weep. God is always honest, and doesn't promise instant solutions to deep human hurt. Rather, he says, "I know you're hurting, but I'm with you; for now, that is all you need."

More than that, he offers us hope. No matter how bleak our world may have become, and how unimaginable and distant healing may now feel, he assures us: "With my grace you will get through this. Trust me."

For some, who have undergone the especially wrenching death of a child or experienced the shock of a sudden or otherwise untimely loss, there's a special need for answers. "Why, God?" Or, if we're honest, "What kind of God are you who'll let this happen?" We may fear either that God is not as loving or as powerful as we'd thought: did this death happen because God didn't want to act, or was unable to?

So we need reassurance that we serve a God big enough to hear our most anguished, and even most angry, cries. The God to whom Job turned in the Old Testament is the same God we serve today, and the mystery of agony and loss that Job underwent ultimately needs the same resolution in our lives that he found: God is all knowing, all powerful, all loving, and he can be trusted to take care of those pieces we cannot understand.

Finally, there is his promise of eternal life for those we have lost and, eventually, for ourselves as well. We have it on the authority of Jesus himself that heaven and eternal life are realities. And we have his word that he has gone ahead to prepare a place for us.

Presumably you're looking at this book because you have lost a loved one, and are grappling with the swirl of emotions or even the numbness that come in death's wake. Perhaps what you're going through is making you question the foundations of your faith itself.

But however you're responding to death's intrusion in your life, know that millions upon millions of Christians have traveled this path of grief before you. Drawing upon their experiences and on the insights that God himself has given us, this collection of Scripture verses and quotations from other writers offers you a set of reminders: God comforts, God offers hope, God is indeed in control, and God will one day bring his people home.

The French writer Madame de Stael said "We understand death for the first time when he puts his hand upon one whom we love." This compilation is for those who have felt that heavy hand, so that they may increasingly know the touch and the grace of a God who has defeated even death.

It is such a secret place, the land of tears.

— Antoine de Saint-Exupéry

There is no grief which time does not
lessen and soften.

— Cicero

Even a king is not ashamed to let God see him cry.

— Janusz Korczak

No one ever told me that grief felt so like fear.
The same fluttering in the stomach, the same
restlessness, the yawning. I keep on swallowing.

— C. S. Lewis

The flood of grief decreaseth when it can
swell no longer.

— Francis Bacon

We are healed of a suffering only by
experiencing it to the full.

— Marcel Proust

Not even the most learned philosopher or
theologian knows what [death] is going to be like.
But there is one thing which the simplest Christian
knows—he knows it is going to be all right.

— John Baillie

The grace of God is in my mind shaped like a key,
that comes from time to time and unlocks the
heavy doors.

— Donald Swan

He dared to believe his way through the
deepest gloom.

— Friedrich Zundel, on German pastor Johann Blumhardt

God never gives strength for tomorrow, or for the
next hour, but only for the strain of the minute.

— Oswald Chambers

He said not: thou shalt not be troubled, thou shalt
not be tempted, thou shalt not be distressed. But he
said thou shalt not be overcome.

— Julian of Norwich

I believe in the sun even when it is not shining. I believe in love even when not feeling it. I believe in God even when he is silent.

— Anonymous inscription on the wall of a cellar in
   Cologne, Germany, where Jews hid from the Nazis

Christ came and he did not really explain [suffering]: he did far more. He met it, willed it, transformed it, and he taught us how to do all this, or rather he himself does it within in, if we do not hinder his all-healing hands.

— Friedrich von Hügel

She taught me that grief is a time to be lived through, experienced fully, and that the heavens will not fall if I give voice to my anger against God in such a time.

— Elizabeth Watson

Are there any quotations on the previous few pages that are especially helpful to you? If so, why? Write your answer or reflections here. Use the extra pages at the end if you need more space.

Death is the supreme festival on the road to
freedom.

— Dietrich Bonhoeffer


In the midst of life we are in death.

— Book of Common Prayer


God of all consolation,
in your unending love and mercy for us
you turn the darkness of death
into the dawn of new life.
Be our refuge and strength
to lift us from the darkness of this grief
to the peace and light of your presence.
Your son, our Lord Jesus Christ,
by dying for us, conquered death
and by rising again, restored life.
May we then go forward eagerly to meet him,
and after our life on earth
be reunited with our brothers and sisters
where every tear will be wiped away.

— Prayer for pastoral Care of the Sick

Death cannot sever what the cross unites.

— Unknown

Those who die in grace go no further from us than God—and God is very near.

— Pierre Teilhard de Chardin

The ancients feared death; we, thanks to Christianity, fear only dying.

— Julius and Augustus Hare

Is death the last sleep? No, it is the last and final awakening.

— Sir Walter Scott

Death be not proud, though some have called thee
Mighty and dreadful, for, thou art not so,
For, those, whom thou think'st,
thou doest overthrow,
Die not, poor death, nor yet canst
thou kill me . . . .
One short sleep past, we wake eternally,
And death shall be no more: death, thou shalt die.

— John Donne

If you knew what he knows about death you would
clap your listless hands.

— George MacDonald

Abide with me; fast falls the eventide;
The darkness deepens; Lord with me abide.
When other helpers fail and comforts flee,
Help of the helpless, O abide with me.

— Henry F. Lyte

Death, that final curb on freedom, has itself suffered a death blow through the resurrection of Jesus.

— Michael Green

Death is not the end, it is simply walking out of the physical form and into the spirit realm, which is our true home. It's going back home.

— Stephen Christopher

Do not try to be strong. Just be still and know that he is God, and will sustain you, and bring you through.

— *Streams in the Desert*

Are there any quotations on the previous few pages that are especially helpful to you? If so, why? Write your answer or reflections here. Use the extra pages at the end if you need more space.

Death is but our visible horizon, and our look ought always to be focused beyond it. We should never talk as if death were the end of anything.

— George MacDonald

Death is not a threat to genuine life.
It is but a paper tiger that is no longer free
to terrorize us once we know the truth about
the outcome of the cross. Death is but a
temporary inconvenience that separates our smaller
living from our greater being.

— Calvin Miller

Jesus did not pretend that the past had never happened, but he seemed to find ways of not letting it be the end.

— Celtic Daily Prayer

Death is part of this life and not of the next.

— Elizabeth Bibesco


We should not mourn for our brethren who
have been freed from the world by the divine
summons, since we know that they are not lost, but
only sent on ahead.

— Cyprian, 3rd century bishop of Carthage


Just think of stepping on shore and finding
it heaven!
Of touching a hand and finding it God!
Of breathing new air and finding it celestial!
Of waking up in glory and finding it home!

— L. E. Singer

With death there is the pain of loss, the pain of separation, and there is the promise of eternal life, and the two things can't be separated.

— Frances Dominica

Jesus did not come to explain away suffering or remove it. He came to fill it with his Presence.

— Paul Claudel

If I am in sickness,
my sickness may serve Him;
If I am in sorrow,
my sorrow may serve Him.
He does nothing in vain,
He knows what He is about.

— John Henry Newman

It is idle to grieve if you get no help from grief.

— Seneca

How did Christ defeat death? Not by soaring over it, circumventing it, or denying it, but by going through it. Jesus Christ—the Son of God, the Son of man—was afflicted by the same sorrow, grief, and anguish that deeply wound us in the tragic times of our lives.

— Ron Lee Davis

On this side of the grave we are exiles; on that, citizens; on this side, orphans, on that, children; on this side, captives; on that, freemen.

— Henry Ward Beecher

To a true believer, death is but going to Church: from the Church below to the Church above.

— Augustus Toplady

Are there any quotations on the previous few pages that are especially helpful to you? If so, why? Write your answer or reflections here. Use the extra pages at the end if you need more space.

No believer dies an untimely death. Long life is not
to be reckoned by years as men count them . . . .
There are no untimely figs gathered into God's
basket. The great master of the vineyard plucks the
grapes when they are ripe and ready to be taken,
and not before.

— Charles Haddon Spurgeon




To hurry pain is to leave a classroom still in session.
To prolong pain is to remain seated in a vacated
classroom and miss the next lesson.

— Yahia Labadi




When the day that he must go hence was come,
many accompanied him to the riverside, into which
as he went he said: "Death, where is thy sting"
And as he went down deeper, he said: "Grave,
where is thy victory?" So he passed over, and all the
trumpets sounded for him on the other side.

— John Bunyan, *The Pilgrim's Progress*

"Who gathered this flower?" The gardener
answered, "The Master." And his fellow-servant
held his peace.

— Epitaph in Budock Churchyard and elsewhere


Each day is a day's march nearer home, until in the
end camp in this world is forever struck and
exchanged for permanent residence in the world of
glory.

— William Barclay


I can only tell you what I have felt to be the only
thing which makes life endurable at a time of real
sorrow—God himself. He comes unutterably near
in trouble. In fact, one scarcely knows he exists until
one loves or sorrows. There is no "getting
over" sorrow. I hate the idea. But there is a "getting
into" sorrow, and finding right in the heart of it
the dearest thing of all human beings—the Man of
Sorrows, a God.

— Forbes Robinson

When death separates us from someone we love there is a time when we think no one has suffered as we have. But grief is universal. The method of handling grief is personal and universal.

— Billy Graham

We picture death as coming to destroy; let us rather picture Christ as coming to save. We think of death as ending; let us rather think of life as beginning, and that more abundantly. We think of losing; let us think of gaining. We think of parting; let us think of meeting. We think of going away; let us think of arriving. And as the voice of death whispers, "You must go from earth," let us hear the voice of Christ saying, "You are but coming to Me!"

— Norman Macleod

Since the hole is so enormous and your anguish so deep, you will always be tempted to flee from it. There are two extremes to avoid: being completely absorbed in your pain and being distracted by so many things that you stay away from the wound you want to heal.

— Henri Nouwen

Only when grief finds its work done can God dispense us from it.

— Henri Amiel

Death is awful, demonic . . . What I need to hear from you is that you recognize how painful it is . . . To comfort me you have to come close. Come sit beside me on my mourning bench.

— Nicholas Wolterstorff

Are there any quotations on the previous few pages that
are especially helpful to you? If so, why? Write your
answer or reflections here. Use the extra pages at the end
if you need more space.

Tears may be the beginning, but they should not be the end of things.

— Eleanor Farjeon

Bereavement is the sharpest challenge to our trust in God; if faith can overcome this, there is no mountain which it cannot remove.

— William R. Inge

Suffering passes; having suffered never passes.

— Jean Péguy

The edges of God are tragedy. The depths of God are joy, resurrection, life. Resurrection answers crucifixion; life answers death.

— Marjorie Hewitt Suchocki

There is always a night shift, and sooner or later we
are all put on it.

— Evelyn Underhill


I know well there is no comfort for this pain of
parting: the wound always remains, but one learns
to bear the pain, and learns to thank God for what
he gave, for the beautiful memories of the past, and
the yet more beautiful hope for the future.

— Max Müller


Death has been described as the old family servant
who opens the door to welcome the children home.

— David Watson

Keep up a confidence in Christ, and a dependence
upon him, and he will do what is for the best.
Believe the resurrection, and then be not afraid.

— Matthew Henry

We understand death for the first time when he puts
his hand upon one whom we love.

— Madame de Stael

Because I would not stop for Death
He kindly stopped for me;
The carriage held but just ourselves,
And Immortality.

— Emily Dickinson

Death is as the foreshadowing of life. We die that
we may die no more.

— Herman Hooker

Someday you will read in the papers that D. L. Moody of East Northfield is dead. Don't you believe a word of it. At that moment I shall be more alive than now. I shall have gone up higher, that is all—out of this clay tenement into a house that is immortal; a body that death cannot touch, that sin cannot taint, a body fashioned like unto his glorious body. That which is born of Spirit will live forever.

— D. L. Moody

When peace, like a river, attendeth my way,
When sorrows like sea billows roll;
Whatever my lot, Thou has taught me to say,
It is well, it is well with my soul

— H. G. Spafford (hymn written after the drowning
   of his four daughters during an Atlantic crossing)

Are there any quotations on the previous few pages that are especially helpful to you? If so, why? Write your answer or reflections here. Use the extra pages at the end if you need more space.

Beloved Lena, you will rise and shine like the stars
and the sun. How strange it is to know
that she is at peace and all is well, and yet be
so sorrowful.

— Martin Luther, on the death of his 13-year-old daughter

Death is the golden key that opens the palace
of eternity.

— John Milton

Our Christian faith does not completely explain the
mystery of suffering. It teaches us how to deal with
suffering. It assures us that God does not will
suffering, but he is in it, to redeem it and to turn it
into good and blessing.

— George Appleton

Ye fearful saints, fresh courage take;
The clouds ye so much dread
Are big with mercy, and shall break
In blessings on your head.
His purposes will ripen fast,
Unfolding every hour:
The bud may have a bitter taste,
But sweet will be the flower.
Blind unbelief is sure to err,
And scan his work in vain:
God is his own interpreter
And he will make it plain.

— William Cowper


How else but through a broken heart
May Lord Christ enter in?

— Oscar Wilde


If we believe in Jesus Christ, death for us is union
and reunion, union with him and reunion with
those whom we have loved and lost awhile.

— William Barclay

Through many dangers, toils and snares,
I have already come;
'Tis grace hath brought me safe thus far,
And grace will lead me home.
The Lord has promised good to me,
His Word my hope secures;
He will my Shield and Portion be,
As long as life endures.

— John Newton




Of course! Of course!

— C. S. Lewis, on imagining our response
    after death and arriving in heaven




The grave itself is but a covered bridge, leading
from light to light, through a brief darkness.

— Henry Wadsworth Longfellow

Come to my defense, O God. They're trying to tell me how to grieve. Tell them to leave me alone.

— Unknown

God is closest to those with broken hearts.

— Jewish proverb

Death marks the beginning, not the end. It is our journey to God.

— Billy Graham

Death is nothing at all. It does not count. I have only slipped away into the next room . . . . I am but waiting for you, for an interval, somewhere very near, just round the corner. All is well.

— Henry Scott Holland

Are there any quotations on the previous few pages that are especially helpful to you? If so, why? Write your answer or reflections here. Use the extra pages at the end if you need more space.

43

Those who live in the Lord never see each other for
the last time.

— German proverb


God doesn't pass out "get out of grief free" cards.
God gives us something better: each other.

— Carol Luebering


I do not understand the mystery of grace—only
that it meets us where we are, but does not leave us
where it found us.

— Annie Lamott


Hope is grief's best music.

— Unknown

Earth to earth, ashes to ashes, dust to dust, in sure and certain hope of the resurrection.

— Book of Common Prayer

Grace grows best in winter.

— Samuel Rutherford

I know God will not give me anything I can't handle. I just wish that he didn't trust me so much.

— Mother Teresa

Healing is not forcing the sun to shine, but letting
go of that which blocks the light.

— Stephen and Ondrea Levine

All we go down to the dust; and weeping
over the grave, we make our song: Alleluia,
alleluia, alleluia.

— Orthodox liturgy, thirteenth century

Grief is, in part, confusion and anxiety about how
to advance, how to keep living the story of life
without this important person in the drama. We
don't know what to say or what to do. Life stands
still. The work of grief is to gather the fragments
and to rewrite the narrative, this time minus a
treasured presence.

— Thomas Long

No funeral gloom, my dears, when I am gone,
Corpse gazings, tears, black raiment,
graveyard grimness;
Think of me as withdrawn into the dimness,
Yours still, you mine; remember all the best
Of our past moments, and forget the rest;
And so, to where I wait, come gently on.

— William Allingham

No one really understands the grief or joy of
another.

— Franz Schubert

Death for the Christian is a turning off the light
because the dawn has come.

— Leon Jaworski

Are there any quotations on the previous few pages that are especially helpful to you? If so, why? Write your answer or reflections here. Use the extra pages at the end if you need more space.

**Scripture verses are from the *New International Version*, unless noted otherwise.**

Be strong and courageous. Do not be terrified; do not be discouraged, for the LORD your God will be with you wherever you go.

— Joshua 1:9

Naked I came from my mother's womb, and naked I will depart. The Lord gave and the Lord has taken away; may the name of the Lord be praised.

— Job 1:21

My soul is in anguish.
How long, O LORD, how long?
Turn, O LORD, and deliver me;
save me because of your unfailing love.

— Psalm 6:3-4

Even though I walk through the valley
of the shadow of death, I will fear no evil,
for you are with me; your rod and your staff,
they comfort me.

— Psalm 23:4




You, Lord, keep my lamp burning; my God turns
my darkness into light.

— Psalm 18:28




Turn to me and be gracious to me,
for I am lonely and afflicted.
The troubles of my heart have multiplied;
free me from my anguish.

— Psalm 25:16-17

Weeping may stay for the night,
but rejoicing comes in the morning.

— Psalm 30:5

The Lord is close to the brokenhearted and saves
those who are crushed in spirit.

— Psalm 34:18

God is our refuge and strength,
an ever-present help in trouble.

— Psalm 46:1

Be still, and know that I am God;
I will be exalted among the nations,
I will be exalted in the earth.

— Psalm 46:10

When I am afraid, I will trust in you.
In God, whose word I praise,
in God I trust; I will not be afraid.

— Psalm 56:3-4

God, be gracious to me; be gracious, for I have made you my refuge. I shall seek refuge in the shadow of your wings until the storms are past.

— Psalm 57:1 (Revised English Bible)

Blessed is the Lord: he carries us day by day, God our salvation.

— Psalm 68:19 (Revised English Bible)

Are there any quotations on the previous few pages that are especially helpful to you? If so, why? Write your answer or reflections here. Use the extra pages at the end if you need more space.

55

Your righteousness reaches to the skies, O God,
you who have done great things.
Who, O God, is like you?
Though you have made me see troubles,
many and bitter,
you will restore my life again;
from the depths of the earth you will again
bring me up.
You will increase my honor
and comfort me once again.

— Psalm 71:19-21




Precious in the sight of the LORD
is the death of his faithful servants.

— Psalm 116:15




My soul is weary with sorrow;
strengthen me according to your word.

— Psalm 119:28

I lift up my eyes to the hills —
where does my help come from?
My help comes from the LORD,
the Maker of heaven and earth.
He will not let your foot slip —
he who watches over you will not slumber;
indeed, he who watches over Israel
will neither slumber nor sleep.
The LORD watches over you —
the LORD is your shade at your right hand;
the sun will not harm you by day,
nor the moon by night.
The LORD will keep you from all harm —
he will watch over your life;
the LORD will watch over your coming and going
both now and forevermore.

— Psalm 121

Out of the depths I cry to you, O LORD;
O Lord, hear my voice.
Let your ears be attentive
to my cry for mercy.
I wait for the LORD, my soul waits,
and in his word I put my hope.
My soul waits for the Lord
more than watchmen wait for the morning,
more than watchmen wait for the morning.

— Psalm 130:1-2, 5-6

The LORD is near to all who call on him,
to all who call on him in truth.

— Psalm 145:18

He heals the brokenhearted and binds up
their wounds.

— Psalm 147:3-4

Do you not know? Have you not heard?
The LORD is the everlasting God,
the Creator of the ends of the earth.
He will not grow tired or weary,
and his understanding no one can fathom.
He gives strength to the weary
and increases the power of the weak.
Even youths grow tired and weary,
and young men stumble and fall;
but those who hope in the LORD
will renew their strength.
They will soar on wings like eagles;
they will run and not grow weary,
they will walk and not be faint.

— Isaiah 40:28-31

For I am the LORD, your God,
who takes hold of your right hand
and says to you, Do not fear; I will help you.

— Isaiah 41:13

Are there any quotations on the previous few pages that are especially helpful to you? If so, why? Write your answer or reflections here. Use the extra pages at the end if you need more space.

When you pass through the waters,
I will be with you;
and when you pass through the rivers,
they will not sweep over you.
When you walk through the fire,
you will not be burned;
the flames will not set you ablaze.

— Isaiah 43:2

"For I know the plans I have for you," declares the
LORD, "plans to prosper you and not to harm you,
plans to give you hope and a future."

— Jeremiah 29:11

Because of the LORD's great love we are not
consumed, for his compassions never fail.
They are new every morning; great is your
faithfulness. I say to myself, "The LORD is my
portion; therefore I will wait for him."
The LORD is good to those whose hope is in him,
to the one who seeks him; it is good to wait quietly
for the salvation of the LORD.

— Lamentations 3:22-26

Though he brings grief, he will show compassion,
so great is his unfailing love.
For he does not willingly bring affliction
or grief to the children of men.

— Lamentations 3:32-33

The LORD is a sure protection in time of trouble,
and cares for all who make him their refuge.

— Nahum 1:7 (Revised English Bible)

Though the fig tree does not bud
and there are no grapes on the vines,
though the olive crop fails
and the fields produce no food,
though there are no sheep in the pen
and no cattle in the stalls,
yet I will rejoice in the LORD ,
I will be joyful in God my Savior.

— Habakkuk 3:17-18

Blessed are those who mourn, for they will
be comforted.

— Matthew 5:4

Come to me, all who are weary and whose load is
heavy; I will give you rest.

— Matthew 11:28 (Revised English Bible)

Very truly I tell you, whoever obeys my word will
never see death.

— John 8:51

Jesus said to her, "I am the resurrection and the
life. He who believes in me will live, even though he
dies; and whoever lives and believes in me will
never die."

— John 11:25-26

Do not let your hearts be troubled. Trust in God;
trust also in me. In my Father's house are many
rooms; if it were not so, I would have told you. I
am going there to prepare a place for you. And if
I go and prepare a place for you, I will come back
and take you to be with me that you also may be
where I am. You know the way to the place where I
am going.

— John 14:1-4

Are there any quotations on the previous few pages that are especially helpful to you? If so, why? Write your answer or reflections here. Use the extra pages at the end if you need more space.

Peace I leave with you; my peace I give you. I do not give to you as the world gives. Do not let your hearts be troubled and do not be afraid.

— John 14:27

And we know that in all things God works for the good of those who love him, who have been called according to his purpose.

— Romans 8:28

For I am convinced that neither death nor life, neither angels nor demons, neither the present nor the future, nor any powers, neither height nor depth, nor anything else in all creation, will be able to separate us from the love of God that is in Christ Jesus our Lord.

— Romans 8:38-39

No eye has seen,
no ear has heard,
no mind has conceived
what God has prepared for those who love him.

— 1 Corinthians 2:9

And when this perishable body has been clothed
with the imperishable and our mortality has been
clothed with immortality, then the saying of
scripture will come true: "Death is swallowed up;
victory is won!" "O Death, where is your victory? O
Death, where is your sting?"

— 1 Corinthians 15:54-55 (Revised English Bible)

Thank God, the Father of our Lord Jesus Christ,
that he is our Father and the source of all mercy
and comfort. For he gives us comfort in our trials
so that we in turn may be able to give the same sort
of sympathy to others in theirs.

— 2 Corinthians 1:3-4 (Phillips)

But he said to me, "My grace is sufficient for you, for my power is made perfect in weakness." Therefore I will boast all the more gladly about my weaknesses, so that Christ's power may rest on me.

— 2 Corinthians 12:9

Let us then approach the throne of grace with confidence, so that we may receive mercy and find grace to help us in our time of need.

— Hebrews 4:16

Brothers, we do not want you to be ignorant about those who fall asleep, or to grieve like the rest of men, who have no hope. We believe that Jesus died and rose again and so we believe that God will bring with Jesus those who have fallen asleep in him.

— 1 Thessalonians 4:13-14

Unload all your worries on to him, since he is looking after you.

— 1 Peter 5:7 (Jerusalem)

He will wipe every tear from their eyes. There will be no more death or mourning or crying or pain, for the old order of things has passed away.

— Revelation 21:4

Are there any quotations on the previous few pages that are especially helpful to you? If so, why? Write your answer or reflections here.

Consider writing a letter to the person (or persons) whose loss you are grieving. What would you like the recipient (or recipients) to know about your grief? Use the next several pages to do that.

As we come to the end of these thoughts on grief, there is
perhaps no better way to conclude than with the words that
the Lord said Aaron and his sons should use in blessing
the Israelites:


"Say to them:
'The Lord bless you
    and keep you;
the Lord make his face shine on you
    and be gracious to you;
the Lord turn his face toward you
    and give you peace.'"


—Numbers 6:22-26


Hold these words close, and go in God's peace.

www.ingramcontent.com/pod-product-compliance
Lightning Source LLC
Chambersburg PA
CBHW052220150726
48002CB00003B/1198